CHEETAHS

Published by Creative Education, Inc., 123 South Broad Street, Mankato, Minnesota
56001

Library of Congress Cataloging-in-Publication Data

Wood, Linda C., 1945-
Cheetahs / by Linda C. Wood and Cynthia L. Jenson.
p.   cm. — (Zoobooks)
Summary: Discusses the habits and behavior of cheetahs and presents several cheetah-
related activities.
ISBN 0-88682-417-6
1. Cheetahs—Juvenile literature. [1. Cheetahs.] I. Jenson, Cynthia L. II. Title. III.
Series: Zoo books (Mankato, Minn.)
QL737.C23W66   1991   599.74'428—dc20   91-9828 CIP AC

CHEETAHS

Zoobook Series Created by
John Bonnett Wexo

Written by
Linda C. Wood
Cynthia L. Jenson

Zoological Consultant
Charles R. Schroeder, D.V.M.
Director Emeritus
San Diego Zoo &
San Diego Wild Animal Park

Scientific Consultants
Donald Linburg, Ph.D.
Behaviorist
Zoological Society of San Diego

Susan Miller
Research Supervisor
Zoological Society of San Diego

Creative Education

Art Credits

Page Eight: Lower Left, Walter Stuart; **Upper Right,** Rob MacIntosh; **Pages Eight and Nine:** Walter Stuart, **Page Nine: Lower Right and Lower Left,** Rob MacIntosh; **Pages Ten and Eleven:** Walter Stuart; **Top,** Mike Meaker; **Page Eleven: Lower Right,** Rob MacIntosh; **Pages Twelve and Thirteen:** Walter Stuart; **Pages Sixteen and Seventeen:** Chuck Ripper; **Page Seventeen: Bottom,** Walter Stuart; **Pages Eighteen and Nineteen:** Chuck Ripper; **Page Eighteen: Lower Left,** Walter Stuart; **Page Nineteen: Lower Right,** Chuck Ripper; **Activities Art:** Elizabeth Morales-Denney.

Photographic Credits

Front Cover: Stephen Krasemann (Allstock); **Pages Six and Seven:** Jen and Des Bartlett (Bruce Coleman, Ltd.); **Page Eight:** Cristina Smith (Wildlife Education, Ltd.); **Page Nine:** David Madison (Bruce Coleman, Inc.); **Page Ten:** Gunter Ziesler (Bruce Coleman, Ltd.); **Page Eleven: Upper Right,** David Madison (Bruce Coleman, Inc.); **Lower Middle,** Cristina Smith (Wildlife Education, Ltd.); **Page Twelve: Upper Right,** K. Ammann; **Middle Left,** Y. Arthus-Bertrand (Ardea London); **Page Thirteen: Upper Right,** K. Ammann (Bruce Coleman, Inc.); **Lower Right,** Joe MacDonald (Tom Stack and Associates); **Pages Fourteen and Fifteen:** Mark Boulton (Bruce Coleman, Ltd,); **Page Sixteen:** Art Resource, New York; **Page Seventeen: Upper Middle,** B. Gozzoli (Art Resource, New York; **Lower Left,** Riley Caton (Allstock); **Page Eighteen:** Peter Pickford (DRK Photo); **Page Nineteen: Middle Right,** Ron Garrison (Zoological Society of San Diego); **Lower Left,** Steve Raymer (National Geographic Society); **Pages Twenty and Twenty-one:** Gunter Ziesler (Bruce Coleman, Ltd.); **Page Twenty-two: Upper Left,** Stephen J. Krasemann (DRK Photo); **Upper Right and Lower Left,** Cristina Smith (Wildlife Education, Ltd.); **Page Twenty-three:** Cristina Smith (Wildlife Education, Ltd.).

Our Thanks To: Kurt Johnson and Nina Marshall (TRAFFIC); Bonnie Chapin (International Wildlife Coalition); Bonnie Becker (Metropolitan Museum of Art); Diane Dodsworth (Helen Woodward Animal Care Center); Blaire Van Valkenburgh, Ph.D. (UCLA); George T. Jefferson, Ph.D. (The Page Museum); Larry Martin, Ph.D. (University of Kansas); Richard Parsons (Fur Information Council of America); Linda Coates, Valerie Hare, and Wendy Perkins (San Diego Zoo Library); Jane Kimber (Bruce Castle Museum); Karl and Katherine Ammann; Nan Wrogemann; Darrel Plowes; Peter Rice; Carrie Thulin; Tara Epstein; Wendy Duncan; Tracy Lewis; Tyler Burch; Erika Smith; Daniel Martin; Chris Elliott; Joe Selig.

Contents

Cheetahs are the fastest animals on land—able to reach speeds of up to 70 miles per hour (113 kilometers per hour) for short distances. And because of their long legs, slender bodies, and beautiful spots, many people consider them to be the most elegant of all cats. One glance at the cheetah at right, and it's easy to see why.

Scientists classify cheetahs as part of the animal group known as big cats. Others in this group include lions, tigers, leopards, jaguars, snow leopards, and clouded leopards. Like all of these cats, cheetahs are meat eaters, or *carnivores* (KAR-nuh-vorz). But they differ from the other big cats in three important ways.

First of all, cheetahs aren't nearly as powerful as other big cats. Lions, tigers, and jaguars, for example, have incredibly strong bodies and powerful jaws to help them catch prey and fight off enemies. But the smaller cheetah must rely on speed alone for its survival.

Second, cheetahs are the only members of the big cat family that cannot roar. They can purr, however, and purr they do—just like house cats, but at a much greater volume! Scientists who study cheetahs in the wild have discovered that they usually purr the loudest while grooming each other or when resting together.

Finally, cheetahs are the most gentle of the big cats. They rarely squabble, even among themselves, and would rather run away than fight. Unfortunately, this trait, which makes cheetahs so appealing to us, has made it very hard for them to survive in the wild. Because they *aren't* fighters by nature, other predators take advantage of them. They steal their food, eat their cubs, and even attack the adults! For this reason, cheetahs in the wild live only 4 to 5 years. But in captivity, where they are safe from predators, they can live for up to 15 years.

One million years ago, the ancestors of cheetahs roamed all over Europe, Asia, North America, and Africa. But today cheetahs can be found only in Africa and in very small numbers in Asia. Their favorite habitats are dry grasslands, woodlands, and bushlands. In these areas, they can take advantage of the wide open spaces for chasing prey.

Unfortunately, these open ranges are fast disappearing and cheetahs are highly endangered. If we are to save these beautiful animals from extinction, we must act fast!

The young cheetah at right is about 9 months old.

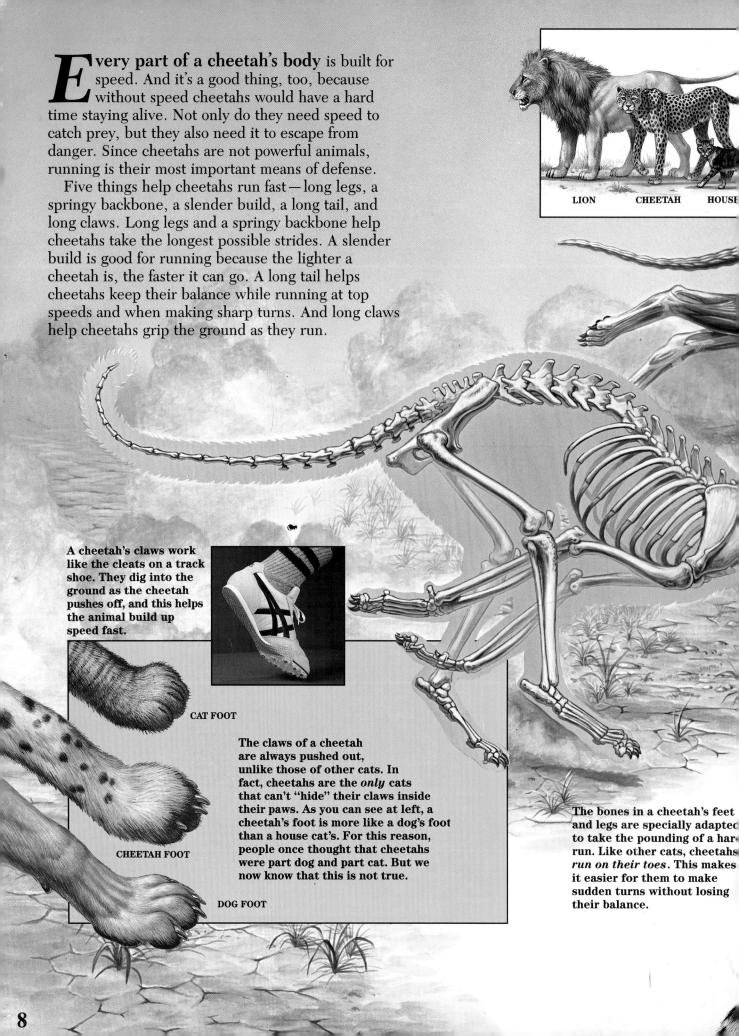

Every part of a cheetah's body is built for speed. And it's a good thing, too, because without speed cheetahs would have a hard time staying alive. Not only do they need speed to catch prey, but they also need it to escape from danger. Since cheetahs are not powerful animals, running is their most important means of defense.

Five things help cheetahs run fast — long legs, a springy backbone, a slender build, a long tail, and long claws. Long legs and a springy backbone help cheetahs take the longest possible strides. A slender build is good for running because the lighter a cheetah is, the faster it can go. A long tail helps cheetahs keep their balance while running at top speeds and when making sharp turns. And long claws help cheetahs grip the ground as they run.

LION   CHEETAH   HOUSE

A cheetah's claws work like the cleats on a track shoe. They dig into the ground as the cheetah pushes off, and this helps the animal build up speed fast.

CAT FOOT

CHEETAH FOOT

DOG FOOT

The claws of a cheetah are always pushed out, unlike those of other cats. In fact, cheetahs are the *only* cats that can't "hide" their claws inside their paws. As you can see at left, a cheetah's foot is more like a dog's foot than a house cat's. For this reason, people once thought that cheetahs were part dog and part cat. But we now know that this is not true.

The bones in a cheetah's feet and legs are specially adapted to take the pounding of a hard run. Like other cats, cheetahs *run on their toes*. This makes it easier for them to make sudden turns without losing their balance.

8

hough cheetahs are big
s, next to a male lion a
etah looks pretty small.
 compared to a house
, a cheetah seems huge!
 average cheetah is
et long (2.1 meters),
uding its tail.
 it weighs about
 pounds (57
grams).

With their long legs and springy backbones, cheetahs can take very long steps—and so they can
cover a lot of ground. When moving at top speed, a
cheetah can cover as many as 20 feet (6.1 meters)
in one stride! A horse, which is a much bigger animal, has a stride of only about 25 feet (7.6 meters).

der their
n, cheetahs look
narkably like house
ts. But they have longer legs
n most cats. They have smaller
ads. And they have leaner, more
scular bodies. All of these features
ke cheetahs the most streamlined—
d the fastest—of all cats.

Cheetahs can build up speed, or *accelerate*, at an incredible rate. This enables
them to outrun all other animals over
short distances. From a standing start, a
cheetah can accelerate to 45 miles per
hour (72 kilometers per hour) in just
2 seconds! Most racing cars can't do that!

One way you can tell a cheetah from
other spotted cats is by the dark lines
that run from its eyes to its mouth. Called
"tear lines," these dark areas may help to
protect the cheetah's eyes from the glare
of the sun. Similarly, football players
rub black grease under their eyes to cut
down the sun's glare during games.

9

Cheetahs are wonderful hunters. Unlike other cats, which hunt by creeping up close to their prey and then pouncing on it, cheetahs usually run their prey down at high speeds — sometimes from as far away as 300 feet (91 meters). But when tall grass is available, cheetahs will also stalk their prey. And at these times, their spotted coats and golden color help to hide them.

Cheetahs do most of their hunting in the cool early morning or late afternoon hours. And usually they hunt alone. But as you will see, families of cheetahs — a mother and her cubs or a group of males — may also hunt together. Their favorite prey are gazelles, impalas, and other small antelopes.

When a cheetah can't find enough of its regular prey, it will go after ostriches, hares, birds, lizards, and frogs. Cheetahs will also eat bird eggs and even fruit. An African fruit called the tsama (TZAH-muh) melon is a special favorite during dry weather because it contains lots of water.

OSTRICH

BIR

EGGS

SPRINGHARE

After chasing its prey at lightning speed the cheetah strikes the animal on the ru to knock it over. It will then hold the pre by the throat to cut off its air supply. As incredible as it seems, the whole chase l only 20 seconds — yet it may cover as ma as 550 feet (168 meters).

Cheetahs hunt almost completely by sight. To look for prey, they usually climb on top of a termite mound or other elevated place to get a good view of the plains. Once they've spotted a herd, they single out a victim — and the hunt is on. This mother and her grown cubs are looking for prey together. The mother will probably make the catch. Then the whole family will share the meal.

GUINEA FOWL

FROG

LIZARD

MELON

Even though cheetahs are very good hunters, they don't always catch the animals they go after. They tire quickly, and if they can't catch the prey within a few hundred feet, they give up the chase. For this reason, only about half of all cheetah hunts are successful.

After making a kill, cheetahs usually drag their prey into the shade of a bush or tree. But they don't eat it right away. They must catch their breath first. After a hard chase, even the hungriest cheetah may need to rest for up to 30 minutes before beginning to eat!

RASP

To scrape the last bit of meat off of bones, cheetahs have very rough tongues. In fact, a cheetah's tongue is almost as rough as a rasp — a rough-surfaced tool that is used to file wood. If you've ever been licked by a house cat, then you know how rough a cat's tongue can be. A cheetah's tongue is even rougher than that!

Cheetah mothers take very good care of their babies. As soon as the babies are born, a cheetah mother nestles them close to her to keep them warm. She feeds them milk and, except when she goes hunting, she almost never lets them out of her sight. If they do begin to stray, she calls them back by purring or by making a soft "chirping" sound.

Cheetah babies, called *cubs*, need this kind of protection because lions, hyenas, and other predators will eat them if they have a chance. For this reason, the cubs must stay very close to their mothers at all times. In fact, for almost 2 years after they are born, cheetah cubs do almost everything with their families. During this time, they have a lot to learn if they are to hunt and survive on their own.

Cheetah cubs are born in groups, or *litters*, o to eight babies. The average number of cubs litter is four. Cheetah babies are blind at bir And each one weighs less than a pound. The in this picture are only a few days old. Older like the ones at right, have long woolly hair their heads, necks, and backs. They will kee hair until they are about 3 months old.

For the first few weeks of their lives, the cubs feed on the milk that they get from their mothers. After that, they start eating more and more meat. Their mother makes a kill, and then she calls the cubs to come and share it with her.

Grooming is an important part of a cheetah's life. Members of cheetah families spend many hours every day grooming each other with their tongues. And after meals, they all help to clean each other's faces. This older cub is cleaning its mother's face.

Cheetah mothers are very protective of their young. If a hyena or other predator comes too close, the mother will hiss and swat at the animal to warn it to stay away from her babies!

Cheetah cubs grow very fast. As you can see in this picture, by the time they are 3 months old, they are already beginning to look like adult cheetahs. When they are about 6 months old, they will start learning how to hunt. Their mother will teach them, but it will take almost a year and a half for them to be able to hunt on their own.

Cheetah families are very close. Here a cheetah mother and her large cubs rest together after a meal. When cubs lie close together, they often purr very loudly.

Cheetahs and people have always gotten along well. The most shy and gentle of all the wild cats, cheetahs have never been known to attack a human being without cause. They are so gentle, in fact, that people have kept them as pets for thousands of years.

Many cultures, from the Sumerians in 3000 B.C. to the princes of India in the 19th century, used cheetahs for hunting. Noblemen made a sport of "training" cheetahs to hunt animals before an audience. But people didn't really teach cheetahs how to hunt. Historians tell us that it was usually the older cheetahs that were used for this sport—after their mothers had taught them how to hunt.

The ancient Egyptians thought that all cats were sacred—and cheetahs were no exception. This golden cat's head, which shows the typical tear lines of the cheetah, was worn on the cloak of an Egyptian priest around 1370 B.C.

Akbar the Great, an emperor in India around 1550, kept 1,000 cheetahs for hunting a type of gazelle called the black buck. A cheetah was blindfolded with a colorful hood and brought within range of the prey. When the hood was removed, the cheetah would streak after the prey to the cheers of the watching crowd.

Cheetahs were very popular among Italian noblemen of the 15th and 16th centuries. The painting at left shows a cheetah being carried to a hunt on horseback. A trainer, seated on the front of the horse, kept the cheetah in place with a gold chain. When they reached the hunt, the trainer would release the cheetah to chase hares and deer.

People have always admired cheetahs for their great speed. In the 1920s, some people even tried to race cheetahs against greyhounds to see which animal could run the fastest. But the races didn't work out very well, because the cheetahs kept cutting across the track!

Wild animals generally don't make good pets. But for centuries, people have found cheetahs to be gentle and reliable. Some people in Africa keep cheetahs right in their own backyards—and even inside their homes! But even "pet" cheetahs aren't *tame*—they will always be wild.

Cheetahs need our help. Over the last century, the number of cheetahs left in the world has dropped dramatically. Just 100 years ago, an estimated 100,000 cheetahs roamed the grasslands of Africa and Asia. Today only 10,000 survive in Africa, and *fewer than 250 live in Asia!* At that rate, by the year 2000, there may not be any cheetahs left in the wild at all.

One reason cheetahs are dying out is that grasslands are being converted into farms and pastures, and cheetahs have nowhere left to hunt. Another reason is illegal hunting—many cheetahs have been killed for their beautiful spotted skins.

But many people want to save cheetahs. New laws protect cheetahs from hunters. And several zoos are working to help cheetahs build up their numbers in captivity.

In most countries, there are laws against hunting cheetahs. Even illegal hunters, called *poachers* [POE-chers], sometimes chase cheetahs in fast trucks. This mother cheetah has hidden her babies in the brush to keep them safe from poachers.

ASIA

AFRICA

RED SEA

INDIA

Cheetahs once lived in Asia from India to the Red Sea, and in all parts of Africa except tropical forests. In the last century, their range has shrunk rapidly. Cheetahs have vanished from much of Africa, and they are now almost extinct in Asia! The map shows cheetahs' former range, and where they live today.

■ PRESENT RANGE

▨ PAST RANGE

Cheetahs have a hard time surviving, even when people aren't around. Other predators, like this hyena, steal food from these shy cats. Hyenas and lions may take as many as one out of every three cheetah kills. This means that cheetahs must catch more prey animals than they actually need to eat—and extra hunting uses up precious energy.

When people use land for farms or for grazing domestic animals, the range of cheetahs and their prey is reduced. Without enough natural prey, cheetahs may become hungry enough to kill a domestic animal. This makes people afraid—*so* afraid that they may even kill cheetahs.

Cheetahs have always had trouble breeding in captivity. Today, in places such as the San Diego Wild Animal Park, in California, that trend is changing. Scientists are now creating habitats in which cheetahs feel at home raising their young. So far, over 80 cheetahs have been born at the San Diego facility!

Today there are laws preventing people from buying cheetah skins. But despite these laws, cheetah skins are still being sold worldwide. This man has caught people bringing cheetah skins into his country.

In the past, some people thought it was glamorous to wear spotted furs taken from cheetahs. In the early 1970s, hundreds of cheetahs were killed for their fur *every month!* But in recent years, that number has dropped. People are realizing more and more that cheetah fur belongs on cheetahs—not on people.

19

No animal is more graceful than a running cheetah. When a cheetah runs at top speed, it almost seems to be flying through the air. This cheetah is moving so fast that all four of its feet are off the ground!

CHEETAHS ACTIVITIES

Use what you have learned about cheetahs to complete the fun activities on these pages.

Cheetah Cookies

You will need:

1 stick butter
1¼ cups sugar
4 eggs
4 cups flour
1 teaspoon vanilla
Chocolate chips
Butterscotch chips (option
Chocolate sprinkles (optio

Cheetahs On The Move

You have learned that cheetahs are the fastest animals on land. In just 20 seconds, they can run 550 feet (168 meters)! How far can you run in 20 seconds? Mark your starting point with masking tape. Have someone time you while you run for 20 seconds. Then, mark your finish point with tape. Now measure the number of feet between your start and finish points. Compare your distance with that of a cheetah.

Cheetah Mask

Create cheetah faces on yourself or on a friend. Use makeup, colored zinc oxide, or face paint. Remember to make dark tear lines extending from the eye to the upper lip on each side of the face.

k an adult to help you
llow the recipe below.

ash your hands.

eheat an oven to 300°F (150°C).

a large bowl, mix together the butter, sugar, and
nilla. Stir for three minutes, or until the mixture
completely blended. Stir the eggs into the
xture, one at a time.

ld the flour and mix until you can make a ball of
ugh.

eak off small pieces of dough. Mold each piece
o a cheetah face. Add extra flour if the dough is
sticky to handle.

e chocolate chips, butterscotch chips, or
ocolate sprinkles to give your cheetahs eyes,
ts, and tear lines.

ke the cookies on a greased cookie sheet
20 to 25 minutes. Let them cool
fore eating.

Cheetah Secret Code

The numbers below really represent words written in a secret code.
Each letter in the alphabet is represented by a number in the code.
For example, A = 1 and P = 16. Use the secret code to discover
each of the sixteen mystery cheetah words. On a piece of paper,
write the letter that goes with each number.

a.	3	21	2		g.	16	18	5	25	
b.	6	21	18		h.	16	21	18	18	
c.	18	21	14		i.	18	1	14	7	5
d.	3	1	20	19	j.	3	12	1	23	19
e.	16	5	20	19	k.	19	16	15	20	19
f.	20	15	5	19	l.	1	6	18	9	3	1

m. 12 9 20 20 5 18
n. 16 15 1 3 8 5 18 19
o. 16 18 5 4 1 20 15 18
p. 3 1 18 14 9 22 15 18 5

1	2	3	4	5	6	7	8	9	10	11	12	13
A	B	C	D	E	F	G	H	I	J	K	L	M
14	15	16	17	18	19	20	21	22	23	24	25	26
N	O	P	Q	R	S	T	U	V	W	X	Y	Z

Answers

a. cub   c. run   e. pets   g. prey   i. range   k. spots   m. litter   o. predator
b. fur   d. cats   f. toes   h. purr   j. claws   l. Africa   n. poachers   p. carnivore

You can help save endangered cheetahs
by making a poster about them. On the poster, show
how human activities have hurt cheetahs (see pages 12 and 13 for
ideas). Share the poster with your friends, family, and schoolmates.
Be sure to tell them what *they* can do to help save cheetahs from
extinction. Everyone can make a difference!

Kids Can Make A Difference

Index